OECD/G20 Base Erosion and Profit Shifting Project

Preventing the Artificial Avoidance of Permanent Establishment Status, Action 7 - 2015 Final Report

This document and any map included herein are without prejudice to the status of or sovereignty over any territory, to the delimitation of international frontiers and boundaries and to the name of any territory, city or area.

Please cite this publication as:
OECD (2015), *Preventing the Artificial Avoidance of Permanent Establishment Status, Action 7 - 2015 Final Report*, OECD/G20 Base Erosion and Profit Shifting Project, OECD Publishing, Paris.
http://dx.doi.org/10.1787/9789264241220-en

ISBN 978-92-64-24121-3 (print)
ISBN 978-92-64-24122-0 (PDF)

Series: OECD/G20 Base Erosion and Profit Shifting Project
ISSN 2313-2604 (print)
ISSN 2313-2612 (online)

Photo credits: Cover © ninog – Fotolia.com

Corrigenda to OECD publications may be found on line at: *www.oecd.org/about/publishing/corrigenda.htm*.

Foreword

International tax issues have never been as high on the political agenda as they are today. The integration of national economies and markets has increased substantially in recent years, putting a strain on the international tax rules, which were designed more than a century ago. Weaknesses in the current rules create opportunities for base erosion and profit shifting (BEPS), requiring bold moves by policy makers to restore confidence in the system and ensure that profits are taxed where economic activities take place and value is created.

Following the release of the report *Addressing Base Erosion and Profit Shifting* in February 2013, OECD and G20 countries adopted a 15-point Action Plan to address BEPS in September 2013. The Action Plan identified 15 actions along three key pillars: introducing coherence in the domestic rules that affect cross-border activities, reinforcing substance requirements in the existing international standards, and improving transparency as well as certainty.

Since then, all G20 and OECD countries have worked on an equal footing and the European Commission also provided its views throughout the BEPS project. Developing countries have been engaged extensively via a number of different mechanisms, including direct participation in the Committee on Fiscal Affairs. In addition, regional tax organisations such as the African Tax Administration Forum, the *Centre de rencontre des administrations fiscales* and the *Centro Interamericano de Administraciones Tributarias*, joined international organisations such as the International Monetary Fund, the World Bank and the United Nations, in contributing to the work. Stakeholders have been consulted at length: in total, the BEPS project received more than 1 400 submissions from industry, advisers, NGOs and academics. Fourteen public consultations were held, streamed live on line, as were webcasts where the OECD Secretariat periodically updated the public and answered questions.

After two years of work, the 15 actions have now been completed. All the different outputs, including those delivered in an interim form in 2014, have been consolidated into a comprehensive package. The BEPS package of measures represents the first substantial renovation of the international tax rules in almost a century. Once the new measures become applicable, it is expected that profits will be reported where the economic activities that generate them are carried out and where value is created. BEPS planning strategies that rely on outdated rules or on poorly co-ordinated domestic measures will be rendered ineffective.

Implementation therefore becomes key at this stage. The BEPS package is designed to be implemented via changes in domestic law and practices, and via treaty provisions, with negotiations for a multilateral instrument under way and expected to be finalised in 2016. OECD and G20 countries have also agreed to continue to work together to ensure a consistent and co-ordinated implementation of the BEPS recommendations. Globalisation requires that global solutions and a global dialogue be established which go beyond OECD and G20 countries. To further this objective, in 2016 OECD and G20 countries will conceive an inclusive framework for monitoring, with all interested countries participating on an equal footing.

A better understanding of how the BEPS recommendations are implemented in practice could reduce misunderstandings and disputes between governments. Greater focus on implementation and tax administration should therefore be mutually beneficial to governments and business. Proposed improvements to data and analysis will help support ongoing evaluation of the quantitative impact of BEPS, as well as evaluating the impact of the countermeasures developed under the BEPS Project.

Table of contents

Abbreviations and acronyms

BEPS	Base erosion and profit shifting
MNE	Multinational enterprise
OECD	Organisation for Economic Co-operation and Development
PE	Permanent establishment
PPT	Principal Purposes Test

Executive summary

Tax treaties generally provide that the business profits of a foreign enterprise are taxable in a State only to the extent that the enterprise has in that State a permanent establishment (PE) to which the profits are attributable. The definition of PE included in tax treaties is therefore crucial in determining whether a non-resident enterprise must pay income tax in another State.

The *Action Plan on Base Erosion and Profit Shifting* (BEPS Action Plan, OECD, 2013a) called for a review of that definition to prevent the use of certain common tax avoidance strategies that are currently used to circumvent the existing PE definition, such as arrangements through which taxpayers replace subsidiaries that traditionally acted as distributors by *commissionnaire* arrangements, with a resulting shift of profits out of the country where the sales took place without a substantive change in the functions performed in that country. Changes to the PE definition are also necessary to prevent the exploitation of the specific exceptions to the PE definition currently provided for by Art. 5(4) of the OECD Model Tax Convention (2014), an issue which is particularly relevant in the digital economy.

This report includes the changes that will be made to the definition of PE in Article 5 of the OECD Model Tax Convention, which is widely used as the basis for negotiating tax treaties, as a result of the work on Action 7 of the BEPS Action Plan.

Together with the changes to tax treaties proposed in the Report on Action 6 (*Preventing the Granting of Treaty Benefits in Inappropriate Circumstances*, OECD, 2015a), the changes recommended in this report will restore taxation in a number of cases where cross-border income would otherwise go untaxed or would be taxed at very low rates as result of the provisions of tax treaties. Taken together, these tax treaty changes will enable countries to address BEPS concerns resulting from tax treaties, which was a key focus of the work mandated by the BEPS Action Plan.

Artificial avoidance of PE status through *commissionnaire* arrangements and similar strategies

A *commissionnaire* arrangement may be loosely defined as an arrangement through which a person sells products in a State in its own name but on behalf of a foreign enterprise that is the owner of these products. Through such an arrangement, a foreign enterprise is able to sell its products in a State without technically having a permanent establishment to which such sales may be attributed for tax purposes and without, therefore, being taxable in that State on the profits derived from such sales. Since the person that concludes the sales does not own the products that it sells, that person cannot be taxed on the profits derived from such sales and may only be taxed on the remuneration that it receives for its services (usually a commission). A foreign enterprise that uses a *commissionnaire* arrangement does not have a permanent establishment because it is able to avoid the application of Art. 5(5) of the OECD Model Tax

Convention, to the extent that the contracts concluded by the person acting as a *commissionnaire* are not binding on the foreign enterprise. Since Art. 5(5) relies on the formal conclusion of contracts in the name of the foreign enterprise, it is possible to avoid the application of that rule by changing the terms of contracts without material changes in the functions performed in a State. *Commissionnaire* arrangements have been a major preoccupation of tax administrations in many countries, as shown by a number of cases dealing with such arrangements that were litigated in OECD countries. In most of the cases that went to court, the tax administration's arguments were rejected.

Similar strategies that seek to avoid the application of Art. 5(5) involve situations where contracts which are substantially negotiated in a State are not formally concluded in that State because they are finalised or authorised abroad, or where the person that habitually exercises an authority to conclude contracts constitutes an "independent agent" to which the exception of Art. 5(6) applies even though it is closely related to the foreign enterprise on behalf of which it is acting.

As a matter of policy, where the activities that an intermediary exercises in a country are intended to result in the regular conclusion of contracts to be performed by a foreign enterprise, that enterprise should be considered to have a taxable presence in that country unless the intermediary is performing these activities in the course of an independent business. The changes to Art. 5(5) and 5(6) and the detailed Commentary thereon that are included in section A of the report address *commissionnaire* arrangements and similar strategies by ensuring that the wording of these provisions better reflect this underlying policy.

Artificial avoidance of PE status through the specific exceptions in Art. 5(4)

When the exceptions to the definition of permanent establishment that are found in Art. 5(4) of the OECD Model Tax Convention were first introduced, the activities covered by these exceptions were generally considered to be of a preparatory or auxiliary nature.

Since the introduction of these exceptions, however, there have been dramatic changes in the way that business is conducted. This is outlined in detail in the Report on Action 1 (*Addressing the Tax Challenges of the Digital Economy*, OECD, 2015b). Depending on the circumstances, activities previously considered to be merely preparatory or auxiliary in nature may nowadays correspond to core business activities. In order to ensure that profits derived from core activities performed in a country can be taxed in that country, Article 5(4) is modified to ensure that each of the exceptions included therein is restricted to activities that are otherwise of a "preparatory or auxiliary" character. The modifications are found in section B of the report.

BEPS concerns related to Art. 5(4) also arise from what is typically referred to as the "fragmentation of activities". Given the ease with which multinational enterprises (MNEs) may alter their structures to obtain tax advantages, it is important to clarify that it is not possible to avoid PE status by fragmenting a cohesive operating business into several small operations in order to argue that each part is merely engaged in preparatory or auxiliary activities that benefit from the exceptions of Art. 5(4). The anti-fragmentation rule proposed in section B will address these BEPS concerns.

Other strategies for the artificial avoidance of PE status

The exception in Art. 5(3), which applies to construction sites, has given rise to abuses through the practice of splitting-up contracts between closely related enterprises. The Principal Purposes Test (PPT) rule that will be added to the OECD Model Tax Convention as a result of the adoption of the Report on Action 6 (*Preventing the Granting of Treaty Benefits in Inappropriate Circumstances*)[1] will address the BEPS concerns related to such abuses. In order to make this clear, the example put forward in section C of this report will be added to the Commentary on the PPT rule. For States that are unable to address the issue through domestic anti-abuse rules, a more automatic rule will be included in the Commentary as a provision that should be used in treaties that do not include the PPT or as an alternative provision to be used by countries specifically concerned with the splitting-up of contracts issue.

Follow-up, including on issues related to attribution of profits to PEs

The changes to the definition of PE that are included in this report will be among the changes proposed for inclusion in the multilateral instrument that will implement the results of the work on treaty issues mandated by the BEPS Action Plan.

Also, in order to provide greater certainty about the determination of profits to be attributed to the PEs that will result from the changes included in this report and to take account of the need for additional guidance on the issue of attribution of profits to PEs, follow-up work on attribution of profits issues related to Action 7 will be carried on with a view to providing the necessary guidance before the end of 2016, which is the deadline for the negotiation of the multilateral instrument.

Background

1. At the request of the G20, the OECD published the report *Addressing Base Erosion and Profit Shifting* (BEPS Report, OECD, 2013b) in February 2013. The BEPS Report identifies the root causes of BEPS and notes that tax planning leading to BEPS turns on a combination of coordinated strategies. The following paragraph from the BEPS Report relates to the current treaty definition of permanent establishment:

> It had already been recognised way in the past that the concept of permanent establishment referred not only to a substantial physical presence in the country concerned, but also to situations where the non-resident carried on business in the country concerned via a dependent agent (hence the rules contained in paragraphs 5 and 6 of Article 5 of the OECD Model Tax Convention). Nowadays it is possible to be heavily involved in the economic life of another country, *e.g.* by doing business with customers located in that country via the internet, without having a taxable presence therein (such as substantial physical presence or a dependent agent). In an era where non-resident taxpayers can derive substantial profits from transactions with customers located in another country, questions are being raised as to whether the current rules ensure a fair allocation of taxing rights on business profits, especially where the profits from such transactions go untaxed anywhere.

2. Following up on the BEPS Report, the OECD published its BEPS Action Plan in July 2013. The BEPS Action Plan identifies 15 actions to address BEPS in a comprehensive manner and sets deadlines to implement these actions. It deals with avoidance strategies related to the permanent establishment concept as follows:

> ***(ii) Restoring the full effects and benefits of international standards***
>
> ***[…]***
>
> ***The definition of permanent establishment (PE) must be updated to prevent abuses.*** In many countries, the interpretation of the treaty rules on agency-PE allows contracts for the sale of goods belonging to a foreign enterprise to be negotiated and concluded in a country by the sales force of a local subsidiary of that foreign enterprise without the profits from these sales being taxable to the same extent as they would be if the sales were made by a distributor. In many cases, this has led enterprises to replace arrangements under which the local subsidiary traditionally acted as a distributor by "*commissionnaire* arrangements" with a resulting shift of profits out of the country where the sales take place without a substantive change in the functions performed in that country. Similarly, MNEs may artificially fragment their operations among multiple group entities to qualify for the exceptions to PE status for preparatory and ancillary activities.

Action 7 – Prevent the Artificial Avoidance of PE Status

Develop changes to the definition of PE to prevent the artificial avoidance of PE status in relation to BEPS, including through the use of commissionnaire arrangements and the specific activity exemptions. Work on these issues will also address related profit attribution issues.

3. The BEPS Report and the BEPS Action Plan recognise that the current definition of permanent establishment must be changed in order to address BEPS strategies. The BEPS Action Plan also recognises that in the changing international tax environment, a number of countries have expressed a concern about how international standards on which bilateral tax treaties are based allocate taxing rights between source and residence States. The BEPS Action Plan indicates that whilst actions to address BEPS will restore both source and residence taxation in a number of cases where cross-border income would otherwise go untaxed or would be taxed at very low rates, these actions are not directly aimed at changing the existing international standards on the allocation of taxing rights on cross-border income.

4. This report includes the changes that will be made to Article 5 of the OECD Model Tax Convention and the Commentary thereon as a result of the work on Action 7 of the BEPS Action Plan. It should be noted that these changes are prospective only and, as such, do not affect the interpretation of the former provisions of the OECD Model Tax Convention and of treaties in which these provisions are included, in particular as regards the interpretation of existing paragraphs 4 and 5 of Article 5.

A. Artificial avoidance of PE status through *commissionnaire* arrangements and similar strategies

5. A *commissionnaire* arrangement may be loosely defined as an arrangement through which a person sells products in a given State in its own name but on behalf of a foreign enterprise that is the owner of these products. Through such an arrangement, a foreign enterprise is able to sell its products in a State without having a permanent establishment to which such sales may be attributed for tax purposes; since the person that concludes the sales does not own the products that it sells, it cannot be taxed on the profits derived from such sales and may only be taxed on the remuneration that it receives for its services (usually a commission).

6. BEPS concerns arising from *commissionnaire* arrangements may be illustrated by the following example, which is based on a court decision that dealt with such an arrangement and found that the foreign enterprise did not have a permanent establishment:

- XCO is a company resident of State X. It specialises in the sale of medical products.
- Until 2000, these products are sold to clinics and hospitals in State Y by YCO, a company resident of State Y. XCO and YCO are members of the same multinational group.
- In 2000, the status of YCO is changed to that of *commissionnaire* following the conclusion of a *commissionnaire* contract between the two companies. Pursuant to the contract, YCO transfers to XCO its fixed assets, its stock and its customer base and agrees to sell in State Y the products of XCO in its own name, but for the account of and at the risk of XCO.
- As a consequence, the taxable profits of YCO in State Y are substantially reduced.

7. Similar strategies that seek to avoid the application of Art. 5(5) involve situations where contracts which are substantially negotiated in a State are not concluded in that State because they are finalised or authorised abroad, or where the person that habitually exercises an authority to conclude contracts constitutes an "independent agent" to which the exception of Art. 5(6) applies even though it is closely related to the foreign enterprise on behalf of which it is acting.

8. It is clear that in many cases *commissionnaire* arrangements and similar strategies were put in place primarily in order to erode the taxable base of the State where sales took place. Changes to the wording of Art. 5(5) and 5(6) are therefore needed in order to address such strategies.

9. As a matter of policy, where the activities that an intermediary exercises in a country are intended to result in the regular conclusion of contracts to be performed by a foreign enterprise, that enterprise should be considered to have a sufficient taxable nexus in that country unless the intermediary is performing these activities in the course of an independent business. The changes to Art. 5(5) and 5(6) and the detailed Commentary that appear below will address *commissionnaire* arrangements and similar strategies by ensuring that the wording of these provisions better reflect this policy. Such changes, however, are not intended to address BEPS concerns related to the transfer of risks between related parties through low-risk distributor arrangements. In these arrangements,

sales generated by a local sales workforce are attributed to a resident taxpayer, which is not the case in the situations that the changes to Art. 5(5) and 5(6) are intended to address. Given this difference, BEPS concerns related to low-risk distributor arrangements are best addressed through the work on Action 9 (Risks and Capital) of the BEPS Action Plan.

CHANGES TO PARAGRAPHS 5 AND 6 OF ARTICLE 5

Replace paragraphs 5 and 6 of Article 5 by the following (changes to the existing text of Article 5 appear in ***bold italics*** *for additions and* ~~strikethrough~~ *for deletions):*

5. Notwithstanding the provisions of paragraphs 1 and 2 ***but subject to the provisions of paragraph 6***, where a person ~~— other than an agent of an independent status to whom paragraph 6 applies —~~ is acting ***in a Contracting State*** on behalf of an enterprise and ~~has, and habitually exercises, in a Contracting State, an authority to conclude contracts~~, ***in doing so, habitually concludes contracts, or habitually plays the principal role leading to the conclusion of contracts that are routinely concluded without material modification by the enterprise, and these contracts are***

a) in the name of the enterprise, ***or***

b) for the transfer of the ownership of, or for the granting of the right to use, property owned by that enterprise or that the enterprise has the right to use, or

c) for the provision of services by that enterprise,

that enterprise shall be deemed to have a permanent establishment in that State in respect of any activities which that person undertakes for the enterprise, unless the activities of such person are limited to those mentioned in paragraph 4 which, if exercised through a fixed place of business, would not make this fixed place of business a permanent establishment under the provisions of that paragraph.

6. ~~An enterprise shall not be deemed to have a permanent establishment in a Contracting State merely because it carries on business in that State through a broker, general commission agent or any other agent of an independent status, provided that such persons are acting in the ordinary course of their business.~~

a) Paragraph 5 shall not apply where the person acting in a Contracting State on behalf of an enterprise of the other Contracting State carries on business in the first-mentioned State as an independent agent and acts for the enterprise in the ordinary course of that business. Where, however, a person acts exclusively or almost exclusively on behalf of one or more enterprises to which it is closely related, that person shall not be considered to be an independent agent within the meaning of this paragraph with respect to any such enterprise.

b) For the purposes of this Article, a person is closely related to an enterprise if, based on all the relevant facts and circumstances, one has control of the other or both are under the control of the same persons or enterprises. In any case, a person shall be considered to be closely related to an enterprise if one possesses directly or indirectly more than 50 per cent of the beneficial interest in the other (or, in the case of a company, more than 50 per cent of

the aggregate vote and value of the company's shares or of the beneficial equity interest in the company) or if another person possesses directly or indirectly more than 50 per cent of the beneficial interest (or, in the case of a company, more than 50 per cent of the aggregate vote and value of the company's shares or of the beneficial equity interest in the company) in the person and the enterprise.

Proposed changes to the Commentary on Article 5

Replace paragraphs 31 to 39 of the Commentary on Article 5 by the following (changes to the existing text of the Commentary appear in ***bold italics*** *for additions and* ~~strikethrough~~ *for deletions):*

Paragraph 5

31. It is a generally accepted principle that an enterprise should be treated as having a permanent establishment in a State if there is under certain conditions a person acting for it, even though the enterprise may not have a fixed place of business in that State within the meaning of paragraphs 1 and 2. This provision intends to give that State the right to tax in such cases. Thus paragraph 5 stipulates the conditions under which an enterprise is deemed to have a permanent establishment in respect of any activity of a person acting for it. ~~The paragraph was redrafted in the 1977 Model Convention to clarify the intention of the corresponding provision of the 1963 Draft Convention without altering its substance apart from an extension of the excepted activities of the person.~~

32. Persons whose activities may create a permanent establishment for the enterprise are ~~so-called dependent agents i.e.~~ persons, whether or not employees of the enterprise, who ***act on behalf of the enterprise and*** are not ***doing so in the course of carrying on a business as an*** independent agent~~s~~ falling under paragraph 6. Such persons may be either individuals or companies and need not be residents of, nor have a place of business in, the State in which they act for the enterprise. It would not have been in the interest of international economic relations to provide that ~~the maintenance of any dependent person~~ ***any person undertaking activities on behalf of the enterprise*** would lead to a permanent establishment for the enterprise. Such treatment is to be limited to persons who in view of ~~the scope of their authority or~~ the nature of their activity involve the enterprise to a particular extent in business activities in the State concerned. Therefore, paragraph 5 proceeds on the basis that only persons ***habitually concluding contracts that are in the name of the enterprise or that are to be performed by the enterprise, or habitually playing the principal role leading to the conclusion of such contracts which are routinely concluded without material modification by the enterprise,*** ~~having the authority to conclude contracts~~ can lead to a permanent establishment for the enterprise ~~maintaining them~~. In such a case the person***'s actions on behalf of the enterprise, since they result in the conclusion of such contracts and go beyond the mere promotion or advertising, are sufficient to conclude that*** ~~has sufficient authority to bind~~ the enterprise~~'s~~ participat***es***~~ion~~ in ***a***~~the~~ business activity in the State concerned. The use of the term "permanent establishment" in this context presupposes, of course, that ***the conclusion of contracts by*** that person***, or as a direct result of the actions of that person,*** ~~makes use of this authority~~ ***takes place*** repeatedly and not merely in isolated cases.

32.1 For paragraph 5 to apply, all the following conditions must be met:

- *a person acts in a Contracting State on behalf of an enterprise;*
- *in doing so, that person habitually concludes contracts, or habitually plays the principal role leading to the conclusion of contracts that are routinely concluded without material modification by the enterprise, and*
- *these contracts are either in the name of the enterprise or for the transfer of the ownership of, or for the granting of the right to use, property owned by that enterprise or that the enterprise has the right to use, or for the provision of services by that enterprise.*

32.2 Even if these conditions are met, however, paragraph 5 will not apply if the activities performed by the person on behalf of the enterprise are covered by the independent agent exception of paragraph 6 or are limited to activities mentioned in paragraph 4 which, if exercised through a fixed place of business, would be deemed not to create a permanent establishment. This last exception is explained by the fact that since, by virtue of paragraph 4, the maintenance of a fixed place of business solely for the purposes of preparatory or auxiliary activities is deemed not to constitute a permanent establishment, a person whose activities are restricted to such purposes should not create a permanent establishment either. Where, for example, a person acts solely as a buying agent for an enterprise and, in doing so, habitually concludes purchase contracts in the name of that enterprise, paragraph 5 will not apply even if that person is not independent of the enterprise as long as such activities are preparatory or auxiliary (see paragraph 22.5 above).

32.3 A person is acting in a Contracting State on behalf of an enterprise when that person involves the enterprise to a particular extent in business activities in the State concerned. This will be the case, for example, where an agent acts for a principal, where a partner acts for a partnership, where a director acts for a company or where an employee acts for an employer. A person cannot be said to be acting on behalf of an enterprise if the enterprise is not directly or indirectly affected by the action performed by that person. As indicated in paragraph 32, the person acting on behalf of an enterprise can be a company; in that case, the actions of the employees and directors of that company are considered together for the purpose of determining whether and to what extent that company acts on behalf of the enterprise.

32.4 The phrase "concludes contracts" focusses on situations where, under the relevant law governing contracts, a contract is considered to have been concluded by a person. A contract may be concluded without any active negotiation of the terms of that contract; this would be the case, for example, where the relevant law provides that a contract is concluded by reason of a person accepting, on behalf of an enterprise, the offer made by a third party to enter into a standard contract with that enterprise. Also, a contract may, under the relevant law, be concluded in a State even if that contract is signed outside that State; where, for example, the conclusion of a contract results from the acceptance, by a person acting on behalf of an enterprise, of an offer to enter into a contract made by a third party, it does not matter that the contract is signed outside that State. In addition, a person who negotiates in a State all elements and details of a contract in a way binding on the enterprise can be said to conclude the contract in that State even if that contract is signed by another person outside that State.

32.5 The phrase "or habitually plays the principal role leading to the conclusion of contracts that are routinely concluded without material modification by the enterprise" is aimed at situations where the conclusion of a contract directly results from the actions that the person performs in a Contracting State on behalf of the enterprise even though, under the relevant law, the contract is not concluded by that person in that State. Whilst the phrase "concludes contracts" provides a relatively well-known test based on contract law, it was found necessary to supplement that test with a test focusing on substantive activities taking place in one State in order to address cases where the conclusion of contracts is clearly the direct result of these activities although the relevant rules of contract law provide that the conclusion of the contract takes place outside that State. The phrase must be interpreted in the light of the object and purpose of paragraph 5, which is to cover cases where the activities that a person exercises in a State are intended to result in the regular conclusion of contracts to be performed by a foreign enterprise, i.e. where that person acts as the sales force of the enterprise. The principal role leading to the conclusion of the contract will therefore typically be associated with the actions of the person who convinced the third party to enter into a contract with the enterprise. The phrase therefore applies where, for example, a person solicits and receives (but does not formally finalise) orders which are sent directly to a warehouse from which goods belonging to the enterprise are delivered and where the enterprise routinely approves these transactions. It does not apply, however, where a person merely promotes and markets goods or services of an enterprise in a way that does not directly result in the conclusion of contracts. Where, for example, representatives of a pharmaceutical enterprise actively promote drugs produced by that enterprise by contacting doctors that subsequently prescribe these drugs, that marketing activity does not directly result in the conclusion of contracts between the doctors and the enterprise so that the paragraph does not apply even though the sales of these drugs may significantly increase as a result of that marketing activity.

32.6 The following is another example that illustrates the application of paragraph 5. RCO, a company resident of State R, distributes various products and services worldwide through its websites. SCO, a company resident of State S, is a wholly-owned subsidiary of RCO. SCO's employees send emails, make telephone calls to, or visit large organisations in order to convince them to buy RCO's products and services and are therefore responsible for large accounts in State S; SCO's employees, whose remuneration is partially based on the revenues derived by RCO from the holders of these accounts, use their relationship building skills to try to anticipate the needs of these account holders and to convince them to acquire the products and services offered by RCO. When one of these account holders is persuaded by an employee of SCO to purchase a given quantity of goods or services, the employee indicates the price that will be payable for that quantity, indicates that a contract must be

concluded online with RCO before the goods or services can be provided by RCO and explains the standard terms of RCO's contracts, including the fixed price structure used by RCO, which the employee is not authorised to modify. The account holder subsequently concludes that contract online for the quantity discussed with SCO's employee and in accordance with the price structure presented by that employee. In this example, SCO's employees play the principal role leading to the conclusion of the contract between the account holder and RCO and such contracts are routinely concluded without material modification by the enterprise. The fact that SCO's employees cannot vary the terms of the contracts does not mean that the conclusion of the contracts is not the direct result of the activities that they perform on behalf of the enterprise, convincing the account holder to accept these standard terms being the crucial element leading to the conclusion of the contracts between the account holder and RCO.

32.7 The wording of subparagraphs a), b) and c) ensures that paragraph 5 applies not only to contracts that create rights and obligations that are legally enforceable between the enterprise on behalf of which the person is acting and the third parties with which these contracts are concluded but also to contracts that create obligations that will effectively be performed by such enterprise rather than by the person contractually obliged to do so.

32.8 A typical case covered by these subparagraphs is where contracts are concluded with clients by an agent, a partner or an employee of an enterprise so as to create legally enforceable rights and obligations between the enterprise and these clients. These subparagraphs also cover cases where the contracts concluded by a person who acts on behalf of an enterprise do not legally bind that enterprise to the third parties with which these contracts are concluded but are contracts for the transfer of the ownership of, or for the granting of the right to use, property owned by that enterprise or that the enterprise has the right to use, or for the provision of services by that enterprise. A typical example would be the contracts that a "commissionnaire" would conclude with third parties under a commissionnaire arrangement with a foreign enterprise pursuant to which that commissionnaire would act on behalf of the enterprise but in doing so, would conclude in its own name contracts that do not create rights and obligations that are legally enforceable between the foreign enterprise and the third parties even though the results of the arrangement between the commissionnaire and the foreign enterprise would be such that the foreign enterprise would directly transfer to these third parties the ownership or use of property that it owns or has the right to use.

32.9 The reference to contracts "in the name of" in subparagraph a) does not restrict the application of the subparagraph to contracts that are literally in the name of the enterprise; it may apply, for example, to certain situations where the name of the enterprise is undisclosed in a written contract.

32.10 The crucial condition for the application of subparagraphs b) and c) is that the person who habitually concludes the contracts, or habitually plays the principal role leading to the conclusion of the contracts that are routinely concluded without material modification by the enterprise, is acting on behalf of an enterprise in such a way that the parts of the contracts that relate to the

transfer of the ownership or use of property, or the provision of services, will be performed by the enterprise as opposed to the person that acts on the enterprise's behalf.

32.11 For the purposes of subparagraph b), it does not matter whether or not the relevant property existed or was owned by the enterprise at the time of the conclusion of the contracts between the person who acts for the enterprise and the third parties. For example, a person acting on behalf of an enterprise might well sell property that the enterprise will subsequently produce before delivering it directly to the customers. Also, the reference to "property" covers any type of tangible or intangible property.

32.12 The cases to which paragraph 5 applies must be distinguished from situations where a person concludes contracts on its own behalf and, in order to perform the obligations deriving from these contracts, obtains goods or services from other enterprises or arranges for other enterprises to deliver such goods or services. In these cases, the person is not acting "on behalf" of these other enterprises and the contracts concluded by the person are neither in the name of these enterprises nor for the transfer to third parties of the ownership or use of property that these enterprises own or have the right to use or for the provision of services by these other enterprises. Where, for example, a company acts as a distributor of products in a particular market and, in doing so, sells to customers products that it buys from an enterprise (including an associated enterprise), it is neither acting on behalf of that enterprise nor selling property that is owned by that enterprise since the property that is sold to the customers is owned by the distributor. This would still be the case if that distributor acted as a so-called "low-risk distributor" (and not, for example, as an agent) but only if the transfer of the title to property sold by that "low-risk" distributor passed from the enterprise to the distributor and from the distributor to the customer (regardless of how long the distributor would hold title in the product sold) so that the distributor would derive a profit from the sale as opposed to a remuneration in the form, for example, of a commission.

~~32.1 Also, the phrase "authority to conclude contracts in the name of the enterprise" does not confine the application of the paragraph to an agent who enters into contracts literally in the name of the enterprise; the paragraph applies equally to an agent who concludes contracts which are binding on the enterprise even if those contracts are not actually in the name of the enterprise. Lack of active involvement by an enterprise in transactions may be indicative of a grant of authority to an agent. For example, an agent may be considered to possess actual authority to conclude contracts where he solicits and receives (but does not formally finalise) orders which are sent directly to a warehouse from which goods are delivered and where the foreign enterprise routinely approves the transactions.~~

33. The ~~authority to conclude~~ contracts ***referred to in paragraph 5*** ~~must~~ cover contracts relating to operations which constitute the business proper of the enterprise. It would be irrelevant, for instance, if the person ~~had authority to~~ ***concluded employment contracts*** ~~engage employees~~ for the enterprise to assist that person's activity for the enterprise or if the person ~~were authorised to~~ conclude***d***, in the name of the enterprise, similar contracts relating to internal

operations only. Moreover, ***whether or not a*** ~~the authority has to be~~ ***person*** habitually ~~exercised~~ ***concludes contracts or habitually plays the principal role leading to the conclusion of contracts that are routinely concluded without material modification by the enterprise*** ~~in the other State;~~should be determined on the basis of the commercial realities of the situation. ~~A person who is authorised to negotiate all elements and details of a contract in a way binding on the enterprise can be said to exercise this authority "in that State", even if the contract is signed by another person in the State in which the enterprise is situated or if the first person has not formally been given a power of representation.~~ The mere fact~~, however,~~ that a person has attended or even participated in negotiations in a State between an enterprise and a client will not be sufficient, by itself, to conclude that the person has ~~exercised in that State an authority to~~ conclude*d* contracts ***or played the principal role leading to the conclusion of contracts that are routinely concluded without material modification by the enterprise*** ~~in the name of the enterprise~~. The fact that a person has attended or even participated in such negotiations could, however, be a relevant factor in determining the exact functions performed by that person on behalf of the enterprise. ~~Since, by virtue of paragraph 4, the maintenance of a fixed place of business solely for purposes listed in that paragraph is deemed not to constitute a permanent establishment, a person whose activities are restricted to such purposes does not create a permanent establishment either.~~

33.1 The requirement that an agent must "habitually" ~~exercise an authority to~~ conclude contracts ***or play the principal role leading to the conclusion of contracts that are routinely concluded without material modification by the enterprise*** reflects the underlying principle in Article 5 that the presence which an enterprise maintains in a Contracting State should be more than merely transitory if the enterprise is to be regarded as maintaining a permanent establishment, and thus a taxable presence, in that State. The extent and frequency of activity necessary to conclude that the agent is "habitually ~~exercising~~" ***concluding contracts or playing the principal role leading to the conclusion of contracts that are routinely concluded without material modification by the enterprise*** ~~contracting authority~~ will depend on the nature of the contracts and the business of the principal. It is not possible to lay down a precise frequency test. Nonetheless, the same sorts of factors considered in paragraph 6 would be relevant in making that determination

34. Where the requirements set out in paragraph 5 are met, a permanent establishment of the enterprise exists to the extent that the person acts for the latter, *i.e.* not only to the extent that such a person ~~exercises the authority to~~ conclude*s* contracts ***or plays the principal role leading to the conclusion of contracts that are routinely concluded without material modification by the enterprise***.~~in the name of the enterprise.~~

35. Under paragraph 5, only those persons who meet the specific conditions may create a permanent establishment; all other persons are excluded. It should be borne in mind, however, that paragraph 5 simply provides an alternative test of whether an enterprise has a permanent establishment in a State. If it can be shown that the enterprise has a permanent establishment within the meaning of paragraphs 1 and 2 (subject to the provisions of paragraph 4), it is not necessary to show that the person in charge is one who would fall under paragraph 5.

35.1 Whilst one effect of paragraph 5 will typically be that the rights and obligations resulting from the contracts to which the paragraph refers will be allocated to the permanent establishment resulting from the paragraph (see paragraph 21 of the Commentary on Article 7), it is important to note that this does not mean that the entire profits resulting from the performance of these contracts should be attributed to the permanent establishment. The determination of the profits attributable to a permanent establishment resulting from the application of paragraph 5 will be governed by the rules of Article 7; clearly, this will require that activities performed by other enterprises and by the rest of the enterprise to which the permanent establishment belongs be properly remunerated so that the profits to be attributed to the permanent establishment in accordance with Article 7 are only those that the permanent establishment would have derived if it were a separate and independent enterprise performing the activities that paragraph 5 attributes to that permanent establishment.

Paragraph 6

36. Where an enterprise of a Contracting State carries on business dealings through ~~a broker, general commission agent or any other agent of~~ an independent ~~status~~ ***agent carrying on business as such***, it cannot be taxed in the other Contracting State in respect of those dealings if the agent is acting in the ordinary course of ~~his~~ ***that*** business (see paragraph 32 above). ~~Although it stands to reason that~~ ***The activities of*** such an agent, ***who*** represent~~sing~~ a separate ***and independent*** enterprise, ~~cannot constitute a~~ ***should not result in the finding of a*** permanent establishment of the foreign enterprise~~, paragraph 6 has been inserted in the Article for the sake of clarity and emphasis~~.

~~37. A person will come within the scope of paragraph 6, i.e. he will not constitute a permanent establishment of the enterprise on whose behalf he acts only if:~~

~~– he is independent of the enterprise both legally and economically, and~~

~~– he acts in the ordinary course of his business when acting on behalf of the enterprise.~~

37. The exception of paragraph 6 only applies where a person acts on behalf of an enterprise in the course of carrying on a business as an independent agent. It would therefore not apply where a person acts on behalf of an enterprise in a different capacity, such as where an employee acts on behalf of her employer or a partner acts on behalf of a partnership. As explained in paragraph 8.1 of the Commentary on Article 15, it is sometimes difficult to determine whether the services rendered by an individual constitute employment services or services rendered by a separate enterprise and the guidance in paragraphs 8.2 to 8.28 of the Commentary on Article 15 will be relevant for that purpose. Where an individual acts on behalf of an enterprise in the course of carrying on his own business and not as an employee, however, the application of paragraph 6 will still require that the individual do so as an independent agent; as explained in paragraph 38.7 below, this independent status is less likely if the activities of that individual are performed exclusively or almost exclusively on behalf of one enterprise or closely related enterprises.

38. Whether a person ***acting as an agent is*** independent of the enterprise represented depends on the extent of the obligations which this person has vis-à-vis the enterprise. Where the person's commercial activities for the enterprise are subject to detailed instructions or to comprehensive control by it, such person cannot be regarded as independent of the enterprise. Another important criterion will be whether the entrepreneurial risk has to be borne by the person or by the enterprise the person represents. ***In any event, the last sentence of subparagraph a) of paragraph 6 provides that in certain circumstances a person shall not be considered to be an independent agent (see paragraphs 38.6 to 38.11 below).*** ~~38.2~~ The following considerations should be borne in mind when determining whether an agent ***to whom that last sentence does not apply*** may be considered to be independent.

38.1 ~~In relation to the test of legal dependence, i~~***I***t should be noted that***, where the last sentence of subparagraph a) of paragraph 6 does not apply because a subsidiary does not act exclusively or almost exclusively for closely related enterprises,*** the control which a parent company exercises over its subsidiary in its capacity as shareholder is not relevant in a consideration of the dependence or otherwise of the subsidiary in its capacity as an agent for the parent. This is consistent with the rule in paragraph 7 of Article 5 ***(see also paragraph 38.11 below)***. ~~But, as paragraph 41 of the Commentary indicates, the subsidiary may be considered a dependent agent of its parent by application of the same tests which are applied to unrelated companies.~~

38.*2*~~3~~ An independent agent will typically be responsible to his principal for the results of his work but not subject to significant control with respect to the manner in which that work is carried out. He will not be subject to detailed instructions from the principal as to the conduct of the work. The fact that the principal is relying on the special skill and knowledge of the agent is an indication of independence.

38.*3*~~4~~ Limitations on the scale of business which may be conducted by the agent clearly affect the scope of the agent's authority. However such limitations are not relevant to dependency which is determined by consideration of the extent to which the agent exercises freedom in the conduct of business on behalf of the principal within the scope of the authority conferred by the agreement.

38.*4*~~5~~ It may be a feature of the operation of an agreement that an agent will provide substantial information to a principal in connection with the business conducted under the agreement. This is not in itself a sufficient criterion for determination that the agent is dependent unless the information is provided in the course of seeking approval from the principal for the manner in which the business is to be conducted. The provision of information which is simply intended to ensure the smooth running of the agreement and continued good relations with the principal is not a sign of dependence.

38.*5*~~6~~ Another factor to be considered in determining independent status is the number of principals represented by the agent. As indicated in paragraph 38.7, independent status is less likely if the activities of the agent are performed wholly or almost wholly on behalf of only one enterprise over the lifetime of the business or a long period of time. However, this fact is not by itself determinative. All the facts and circumstances must be taken into account to determine whether the agent's activities constitute an autonomous business conducted by him in which he bears risk and receives reward through the use of his entrepreneurial skills and knowledge. Where an agent acts for a number of principals in the ordinary course of his business and none of these is predominant in terms of the business carried on by the agent, dependence may exist if the principals act in concert to control the acts of the agent in the course of his business on their behalf.

38.*6*~~7~~ ***An independent agent*** ~~Persons~~ cannot be said to act in the ordinary course of ~~their own~~ ***its*** business ***as such when it performs activities that are unrelated to the business of an agent*** ~~if, in place of the enterprise, such persons perform activities which, economically, belong to the sphere of the enterprise rather than to that of their own business operations~~. Where, for example, a ~~commission agent not only sells the goods or merchandise of the enterprise in his own name but also habitually acts, in relation to that enterprise, as a permanent agent having an authority to conclude contracts, he would be deemed in respect of this particular activity to be a permanent establishment, since he is thus acting outside the ordinary course of his own trade or business (namely that of a commission agent), unless his activities are limited to those mentioned at the end of paragraph 5~~ ***company that acts as a distributor for a number of companies to which it is not closely related also acts as an agent for a closely related enterprise, the activities that the company undertakes as a distributor will not be considered to be part of the activities that the company carries on in the ordinary course of its business as an agent and will therefore not be relevant in determining whether the company is independent from the closely related enterprise on behalf of which it is acting***.

~~38.8 In deciding whether or not particular activities fall within or outside the ordinary course of business of an agent, one would examine the business activities customarily carried out within the agent's trade as a broker, commission agent or other independent agent rather than the other business activities carried out by that agent. Whilst the comparison normally should be made with the activities customary to the agent's trade, other complementary tests may in certain circumstances be used concurrently or alternatively, for example where the agent's activities do not relate to a common trade.~~

38.7 The last sentence of subparagraph a) provides that a person is not considered to be an independent agent where the person acts exclusively or almost exclusively for one or more enterprises to which it is closely related. That last sentence does not mean, however, that paragraph 6 will apply automatically where a person acts for one or more enterprises to which that person is not closely related. Paragraph 6 requires that the person must be carrying on a business as an independent agent and be acting in the ordinary course of that business. Independent status is less likely if the activities of the person are performed wholly or almost wholly on behalf of only one enterprise (or a group of enterprises that are closely related to each other) over the lifetime of that person's business or over a long period of time. Where, however, a person is acting exclusively for one enterprise, to which it is not

closely related, for a short period of time (e.g. at the beginning of that person's business operations), it is possible that paragraph 6 could apply. As indicated in paragraph 38.5, all the facts and circumstances would need to be taken into account to determine whether the person's activities constitute the carrying on of a business as an independent agent.

38.8 The last sentence of subparagraph a) applies only where the person acts "exclusively or almost exclusively" on behalf of closely related enterprises. This means that where the person's activities on behalf of enterprises to which it is not closely related do not represent a significant part of that person's business, that person will not qualify as an independent agent. Where, for example, the sales that an agent concludes for enterprises to which it is not closely related represent less than 10 per cent of all the sales that it concludes as an agent acting for other enterprises, that agent should be viewed as acting "exclusively or almost exclusively" on behalf of closely related enterprises.

38.9 Subparagraph b) explains the meaning of the concept of a "person closely related to an enterprise" for the purpose of the Article. That concept is to be distinguished from the concept of "associated enterprises" which is used for the purposes of Article 9; although the two concepts overlap to a certain extent, they are not intended to be equivalent.

38.10 The first part of subparagraph b) includes the general definition of "a person closely related to an enterprise". It provides that a person is closely related to an enterprise if, based on all the relevant facts and circumstances, one has control of the other or both are under the control of the same persons or enterprises. This general rule would cover, for example, situations where a person or enterprise controls an enterprise by virtue of a special arrangement that allows that person to exercise rights that are similar to those that it would hold if it possessed directly or indirectly more than 50 per cent of the beneficial interests in the enterprise. As in most cases where the plural form is used, the reference to the "same persons or enterprises" at the end of the first sentence of subparagraph b) covers cases where there is only one such person or enterprise.

38.11 The second part of subparagraph b) provides that the definition of "person closely related to an enterprise" is automatically satisfied in certain circumstances. Under that second part, a person is considered to be closely related to an enterprise if either one possesses directly or indirectly more than 50 per cent of the beneficial interests in the other or if a third person possesses directly or indirectly more than 50 per cent of the beneficial interests in both the person and the enterprise. In the case of a company, this condition is satisfied where a person holds directly or indirectly more than 50 per cent of the aggregate vote and value of the company's shares or of the beneficial equity interest in the company.

38.12 The rule in the last sentence of subparagraph a) and the fact that subparagraph b) covers situations where one company controls or is controlled by another company does not restrict in any way the scope of paragraph 7 of Article 5. As explained in paragraph 41.1 below, it is possible that a subsidiary will act on behalf of its parent company in such a way that the parent will be deemed to have a permanent establishment under paragraph 5; if that is the

case, a subsidiary acting exclusively or almost exclusively for its parent will be unable to benefit from the "independent agent" exception of paragraph 6. This, however, does not imply that the parent-subsidiary relationship eliminates the requirements of paragraph 5 and that such a relationship could be sufficient in itself to conclude that any of these requirements are met.

39. According to the definition of the term "permanent establishment" an insurance company of one State may be taxed in the other State on its insurance business, if it has a fixed place of business within the meaning of paragraph 1 or if it carries on business through a person within the meaning of paragraph 5. Since agencies of foreign insurance companies sometimes do not meet either of the above requirements, it is conceivable that these companies do large-scale business in a State without being taxed in that State on their profits arising from such business. In order to obviate this possibility, various conventions concluded by OECD member countries ***before [next update]*** include a provision which stipulates that insurance companies of a State are deemed to have a permanent establishment in the other State if they collect premiums in that other State through an agent established there — other than an agent who already constitutes a permanent establishment by virtue of paragraph 5 — or insure risks situated in that territory through such an agent. The decision as to whether or not a provision along these lines should be included in a convention will depend on the factual and legal situation prevailing in the Contracting States concerned. ***Also, the changes to paragraphs 5 and 6 made in [next update] have addressed some of the concerns that such a provision is intended to address.*** Frequently, therefore, such a provision will not be contemplated. In view of this fact, it did not seem advisable to insert a provision along these lines in the Model Convention.

B. Artificial avoidance of PE status through the specific activity exemptions

10. Art. 5(4) of the OECD Model Tax Convention includes a list of exceptions (the "specific activity exemptions") according to which a permanent establishment is deemed not to exist where a place of business is used solely for activities that are listed in that paragraph.

1. List of activities included in Art. 5(4)

11. The October 2011 and 2012 discussion drafts on the clarification of the PE definition[2] included a proposed change to paragraph 21 of the Commentary on Article 5 according to which, under the current wording of Article 5, paragraph 4 applies automatically where one of the activities listed in subparagraphs *a*) to *d*) is the only activity carried on at a fixed place of business. The Working Group that produced that proposal, however, invited Working Party 1 to examine "whether the conclusion that subparagraphs *a*) to *d*) are not subject to the extra condition that the activities referred therein be of a preparatory or auxiliary nature is appropriate in policy terms". This reflected the views of some delegates who argued that the proposed interpretation did not appear to conform with what they considered to be the original purpose of the paragraph, *i.e.* to cover only preparatory or auxiliary activities.

12. Regardless of the original purpose of the exceptions included in subparagraphs *a*) to *d*) of paragraph 4, it is important to address situations where these subparagraphs give rise to BEPS concerns. It is therefore agreed to modify Art. 5(4) as indicated below so that each of the exceptions included in that provision is restricted to activities that are otherwise of a "preparatory or auxiliary" character. It is also recommended to provide the additional Commentary guidance below which clarifies the meaning of the phrase "preparatory or auxiliary" using a number of examples.

13. Some States, however, consider that BEPS concerns related to Art. 5(4) essentially arise where there is fragmentation of activities between closely related parties and that these concerns will be appropriately addressed by the inclusion of the anti-fragmentation rule in section 2 below. These States therefore consider that there is no need to modify Art. 5(4) as suggested below and that the list of exceptions in subparagraphs *a*) to *d*) of paragraph 4 should not be subject to the condition that the activities referred to in these subparagraphs be of a preparatory or auxiliary character. As indicated in the Commentary below, States that share that view may adopt a different version of Art. 5(4) as long as they include the anti-fragmentation rule referred to in section 2.

MAKING ALL THE SUBPARAGRAPHS OF ART. 5(4) SUBJECT TO A "PREPARATORY OR AUXILIARY" CONDITION

Replace paragraph 4 of Article 5 by the following (changes to the existing text of the paragraph appear in ***bold italics*** *of additions and* ~~*strikethrough*~~ *for deletions):*

4. Notwithstanding the preceding provisions of this Article, the term "permanent establishment" shall be deemed not to include:

a) the use of facilities solely for the purpose of storage, display or delivery of goods or merchandise belonging to the enterprise;

b) the maintenance of a stock of goods or merchandise belonging to the enterprise solely for the purpose of storage, display or delivery;

c) the maintenance of a stock of goods or merchandise belonging to the enterprise solely for the purpose of processing by another enterprise;

d) the maintenance of a fixed place of business solely for the purpose of purchasing goods or merchandise or of collecting information, for the enterprise;

e) the maintenance of a fixed place of business solely for the purpose of carrying on, for the enterprise, any other activity~~ of a preparatory or auxiliary character~~;

f) the maintenance of a fixed place of business solely for any combination of activities mentioned in subparagraphs *a)* to *e)*, ~~provided that the overall activity of the fixed place of business resulting from this combination is of a preparatory or auxiliary character,~~

provided that such activity or, in the case of subparagraph f), the overall activity of the fixed place of business, is of a preparatory or auxiliary character.

Replace paragraphs 21 to 30 of the existing Commentary on Article 5 (changes to the existing text of the Commentary appear in ***bold italics*** *of additions and* ~~*strikethrough*~~ *for deletions):*

Paragraph 4

21. This paragraph lists a number of business activities which are treated as exceptions to the general definition laid down in paragraph 1 and which ~~are not~~, ***when carried on through fixed places of business, are not sufficient for these places to constitute*** permanent establishments~~, even if the activity is carried on through a fixed place of business~~. ***The final part of the paragraph provides that these exceptions only apply if the listed activities have a preparatory or auxiliary character.*** ~~The common feature of these activities is that they are, in general, preparatory or auxiliary activities. This is laid down explicitly in the case of the exception mentioned in~~***Since*** subparagraph ***e) applies to any activity that is not otherwise listed in the paragraph (as long as that activity has a preparatory or auxiliary character), the provisions of the paragraph*** ~~which~~ actually amount~~s~~ to a general restriction of the scope of the definition ***of permanent establishment*** contained in paragraph 1 and, when read with that paragraph, provide a more selective test~~,~~ by which to determine what constitutes a permanent establishment. To a considerable degree***, these provisions*** ~~it~~ limit~~s~~ th***e***~~at~~ definition ***in paragraph 1*** and exclude~~s~~ from its rather wide scope a number of ~~forms of business organisations which, although they are carried on through a fixed place of business~~ ***fixed places of business which, because the business activities exercised through these places are merely preparatory or auxiliary,*** should not be treated as permanent establishments. It is recognised that such a place of business may well contribute to the productivity of the enterprise, but the services it performs are so remote from the actual realisation of profits that it is difficult to allocate any profit to the fixed place of business in question. *[the last two sentences and the last part of the preceding one have been moved from paragraph 23 to this paragraph]* Moreover subparagraph *f)* provides that

combinations of activities mentioned in subparagraphs *a)* to *e)* in the same fixed place of business shall be deemed not to be a permanent establishment, ***subject to the condition, expressed in the final part of the paragraph,*** ~~provided~~ that the overall activity of the fixed place of business resulting from this combination is of a preparatory or auxiliary character. Thus the provisions of paragraph 4 are designed to prevent an enterprise of one State from being taxed in the other State~~,~~ if it ***only*** carries on ~~in that other State,~~ activities of a purely preparatory or auxiliary character in that State. ***The provisions of paragraph 4.1 (see below) complement that principle by ensuring that the preparatory or auxiliary character of activities carried on at a fixed place of business must be viewed in the light of other activities that constitute complementary functions that are part of a cohesive business and which the same enterprise or closely related enterprises carry on in the same State.***

21.1~~24.~~ It is often difficult to distinguish between activities which have a preparatory or auxiliary character and those which have not. The decisive criterion is whether or not the activity of the fixed place of business in itself forms an essential and significant part of the activity of the enterprise as a whole. Each individual case will have to be examined on its own merits. In any case, a fixed place of business whose general purpose is one which is identical to the general purpose of the whole enterprise~~,~~ does not exercise a preparatory or auxiliary activity.

21.2 As a general rule, an activity that has a preparatory character is one that is carried on in contemplation of the carrying on of what constitutes the essential and significant part of the activity of the enterprise as a whole. Since a preparatory activity precedes another activity, it will often be carried on during a relatively short period, the duration of that period being determined by the nature of the core activities of the enterprise. This, however, will not always be the case as it is possible to carry on an activity at a given place for a substantial period of time in preparation for activities that take place somewhere else. Where, for example, a construction enterprise trains its employees at one place before these employees are sent to work at remote work sites located in other countries, the training that takes place at the first location constitutes a preparatory activity for that enterprise. An activity that has an auxiliary character, on the other hand, generally corresponds to an activity that is carried on to support, without being part of, the essential and significant part of the activity of the enterprise as a whole. It is unlikely that an activity that requires a significant proportion of the assets or employees of the enterprise could be considered as having an auxiliary character.

21.3 Subparagraphs a) to e) refer to activities that are carried on for the enterprise itself. A permanent establishment~~, however,~~ ***would therefore*** exist~~s~~ if ***such activities were performed on behalf of other enterprises at the same fixed place of business*** ~~the fixed place of business exercising any of the functions listed in paragraph 4 were to exercise them not only on behalf of the enterprise to which it belongs but also on behalf of other enterprises~~. If, for instance, an ~~advertising agency~~ ***enterprise that maintained an office for the advertising of its own products or services*** were also to engage in advertising ~~for~~ ***on behalf of*** other enterprises ***at that location***, ~~it~~***that office*** would be regarded as a permanent establishment of the enterprise by which it is maintained.

22. Subparagraph *a)* relates ~~only to the case in which an enterprise acquires the use of~~ ***to a fixed place of business constituted by*** facilities ***used by an enterprise*** for storing, displaying or delivering its own goods or merchandise. ***Whether the activity carried on at such a place of business has a preparatory or auxiliary character will have to be determined in the light of factors that include the overall business activity of the enterprise. Where, for example, an enterprise of State R maintains in State S a very large warehouse in which a significant number of employees work for the main purpose of storing and delivering goods owned by the enterprise that the enterprise sells online to customers in State S, paragraph 4 will not apply to that warehouse since the storage and delivery activities that are performed through that warehouse, which represents an important asset and requires a number of employees, constitute an essential part of the enterprise's sale/distribution business and do not have, therefore, a preparatory or auxiliary character.*** ~~Subparagraph b) relates to the stock of merchandise itself and provides that the stock, as such, shall not be treated as a permanent establishment if it is maintained for the purpose of storage, display or delivery. Subparagraph c) covers the case in which a stock of goods or merchandise belonging to one enterprise is processed by a second enterprise, on behalf of, or for the account of, the first mentioned enterprise. The reference to the collection of information in subparagraph d) is intended to include the case of the newspaper bureau which has no purpose other than to act as one of many "tentacles" of the parent body; to exempt such a bureau is to do no more than to extend the concept of "mere purchase".~~

22.1 ***Subparagraph a) would cover, for instance, a bonded warehouse with special gas facilities that an exporter of fruit from one State maintains in another State for the sole purpose of storing fruit in a controlled environment during the custom clearance process in that other State. It would also cover a fixed place of business that an enterprise maintained solely for the delivery of spare parts to customers for machinery sold to those customers. Paragraph 4 would not apply, however, where*** ~~A permanent establishment could also be constituted if~~ an enterprise maintain~~ed~~***s*** a fixed place of business for the delivery of spare parts to customers for machinery supplied to those customers ***and, in addition,*** ~~where, in addition, it~~ ***for the*** maint~~ain~~***enance***~~s~~ or repair~~s~~ ***of*** such machinery, as this ***would*** go~~es~~ beyond the pure delivery mentioned in subparagraph *a)* ~~of paragraph 4~~ ***and would not constitute preparatory or auxiliary activities*** ~~***S***~~since these after-sale ***activities constitute*** ~~organisations perform~~ an essential and significant part of the services of an enterprise vis-à-vis its customers.~~, their activities are not merely auxiliary ones~~ [*the preceding two sentences have been moved from paragraph 25 to this paragraph*].

22.2~~26.1~~***Issues may arise concerning the application of the definition of permanent establishment to*** ~~Another example is that of~~ facilities such as cables or pipelines that cross the territory of a country. Apart from the fact that income derived by the owner or operator of such facilities from their use by other enterprises is covered by Article 6 where ~~they~~***these*** facilities constitute immovable property under paragraph 2 of Article 6, the question may arise as to whether ***subparagraph a)*** ~~paragraph 4~~ applies to them. Where these facilities are used to transport property belonging to other enterprises, subparagraph *a)*, which is restricted to delivery of goods or merchandise belonging to the enterprise that uses the facility, will not be applicable as concerns the owner or operator of these facilities. Subparagraph *e)* also will not be applicable as concerns that enterprise since the cable or pipeline is not used solely for the enterprise and its use is not of preparatory or auxiliary character given the nature of the business of that enterprise. The situation is different, however, where an enterprise owns and operates a cable or pipeline that crosses the territory of a country solely for purposes of transporting its own property and such transport is merely incidental to the business of that enterprise, as in the case of an enterprise that is in the business of refining oil and that owns and operates a pipeline that crosses the territory of a country solely to transport its own oil to its refinery located in another country. In such case, subparagraph *a)* would be applicable. ~~An additional~~***A separate*** question is whether the cable or pipeline could ~~also~~ constitute a permanent establishment for the customer of the operator of the cable or pipeline, *i.e.* the enterprise whose data, power or property is transmitted or transported from one place to another. In such a case, the enterprise is merely obtaining transmission or transportation services provided by the operator of the cable or pipeline and does not have the cable or pipeline at its disposal. As a consequence, the cable or pipeline cannot be considered to be a permanent establishment of that enterprise.

22.3 Subparagraph *b)* relates to the ***maintenance of a stock of goods or merchandise belonging to the enterprise***~~ stock of merchandise itself and provides that the stock, as such, shall not be treated as a permanent establishment if it is maintained for the purpose of storage, display or delivery~~. ***This subparagraph is irrelevant in cases where a stock of goods or merchandise belonging to an enterprise is maintained by another person in facilities operated by that other person and the enterprise does not have the facilities at its disposal as the place where the stock is maintained cannot therefore be a permanent establishment of that enterprise. Where, for example, an independent logistics company operates a warehouse in State S and continuously stores in that warehouse goods or merchandise belonging to an enterprise of State R, the warehouse does not constitute a fixed place of business at the disposal of the enterprise of State R and subparagraph b) is therefore irrelevant. Where, however, that enterprise is allowed unlimited access to a separate part of the warehouse for the purpose of inspecting and maintaining the goods or merchandise stored therein, subparagraph b) is applicable and the question of whether a permanent establishment exists will depend on whether these activities constitute a preparatory or auxiliary activity.***

22.4 Subparagraph *c)* covers the situation~~ case in which~~ ***where*** a stock of goods or merchandise belonging to one enterprise is processed by a second enterprise~~,~~ on behalf of, or for the account of, the first-mentioned enterprise. ***As explained in the preceding paragraph, the mere presence of goods or merchandise belonging to an enterprise does not mean that the fixed place of business where these goods or merchandise are stored is at the disposal of that enterprise. Where, for example, a stock of goods belonging to RCO, an enterprise of State R, is maintained by a toll-manufacturer located in State S for the purposes of processing by that toll-manufacturer, no fixed place of business is at the disposal of RCO and the place where the stock is maintained*** *cannot therefore be a permanent establishment of RCO. If, however, RCO is allowed unlimited access to a separate part of the facilities of the toll-manufacturer for the purpose of inspecting and maintaining the goods stored therein, subparagraph c) will apply and it will be necessary to determine whether the maintenance of that stock of goods by RCO constitutes a preparatory or auxiliary activity. This will be the case if RCO is merely a distributor of products manufactured by other enterprises as in that case the mere maintenance of a stock of goods for the purposes of processing by another enterprise would not form an essential and significant part of RCO's overall activity. In such a case, unless paragraph 4.1 applies, paragraph 4 will deem a permanent establishment not to exist in relation to such a fixed place of business that is at the disposal of the enterprise of State R for the purposes of maintaining its own goods to be processed by the toll-manufacturer.*

22.5 The first part of subparagraph d) relates to the case where premises are used solely for the purpose of purchasing goods or merchandise for the enterprise. Since this exception only applies if that activity has a preparatory or auxiliary character, it will typically not apply in the case of a fixed place of business used for the purchase of goods or merchandise where the overall activity of the enterprise consists in selling these goods and where purchasing is a core function in the business of the enterprise. The following examples illustrate the application of paragraph 4 in the case of fixed places of business where purchasing activities are performed:

- *Example 1: RCO is a company resident of State R that is a large buyer of a particular agricultural product produced in State S, which RCO sells from State R to distributors situated in different countries. RCO maintains a purchasing office in State S. The employees who work at that office are experienced buyers who have special knowledge of this type of product and who visit producers in State S, determine the type/quality of the products according to international standards (which is a difficult process requiring special skills and knowledge) and enter into different types of contracts (spot or forward) for the acquisition of the products by RCO. In this example, although the only activity performed through the office is the purchasing of products for RCO, which is an activity covered by subparagraph d), paragraph 4 does not apply and the office therefore constitutes a permanent establishment because that purchasing function forms an essential and significant part of RCO's overall activity.*
- *Example 2: RCO, a company resident of State R which operates a number of large discount stores, maintains an office in State S during a two-year period for the purposes of researching the local market and lobbying the government for changes that would allow RCO to establish stores in State S. During that period, employees of RCO occasionally purchase supplies for their office. In this example, paragraph 4 applies because subparagraph f) applies to the activities performed through the office (since subparagraphs d) and e) would apply to the purchasing, researching and lobbying activities if each of these was the only activity performed at the*

office) and the overall activity of the office has a preparatory character.

22.6 The second part of subparagraph d) relates to a fixed place of business that is used solely to collect information for the enterprise. An enterprise will frequently need to collect information before deciding whether and how to carry on its core business activities in a State. If the enterprise does so without maintaining a fixed place of business in that State, subparagraph d) will obviously be irrelevant. If, however, a fixed place of business is maintained solely for that purpose, subparagraph d) will be relevant and it will be necessary to determine whether the collection of information goes beyond the preparatory or auxiliary threshold. Where, for example, an investment fund sets up an office in a State solely to collect information on possible investment opportunities in that State, the collecting of information through that office will be a preparatory activity. The same conclusion would be reached in the case of an insurance enterprise that sets up an office solely for the collection of information, such as statistics, on risks in a particular market and in the case of a newspaper bureau set up in a State solely to collect information on possible news stories without engaging in any advertising activities: in both cases, the collecting of information will be a preparatory activity.

23. Subparagraph *e)* ***applies to*** ~~provides that~~ a fixed place of business ***maintained solely for the purpose of carrying on, for the enterprise, any activity that is not expressly listed in subparagraphs a) to d); as long as that activity*** ~~through which the enterprise exercises solely an activity which~~ has ~~for the enterprise~~ a preparatory or auxiliary character, ***that place of business*** is deemed not to be a permanent establishment. The wording of this subparagraph makes it unnecessary to produce an exhaustive list of ~~exceptions~~ ***the activities to which the paragraph may apply, the examples listed in subparagraphs a) to d) being merely common examples of activities that are covered by the paragraph because they often have a preparatory or auxiliary character***. ~~Furthermore, this subparagraph provides a generalised exception to the general definition in paragraph 1~~ *[(the following part of the paragraph has been moved to paragraph 21):* ~~*and, when read with that paragraph, provides a more selective test, by which to determine what constitutes a permanent establishment. To a considerable degree it limits that definition and excludes from its rather wide scope a number of business activities which, although they are carried on through a fixed place of business, should not be treated as permanent establishments. It is recognised that such a place of business may well contribute to the productivity of the enterprise, but the services it performs are so remote from the actual realisation of profits that it is difficult to allocate any profit to the fixed place of business in question.]*~~ ~~Examples are fixed places of business solely for the purpose of advertising or for the supply of information or for scientific research or for the servicing of a patent or a know-how contract, if such activities have a preparatory or auxiliary character.~~ *[that last sentence has been moved to paragraph 23]*

24. ~~It is often difficult to distinguish between activities which have a preparatory or auxiliary character and those which have not. The decisive criterion is whether or not the activity of the fixed place of business in itself forms an essential and significant part of the activity of the enterprise as a whole.~~

~~Each individual case will have to be examined on its own merits. In any case, a fixed place of business whose general purpose is one which is identical to the general purpose of the whole enterprise, does not exercise a preparatory or auxiliary activity~~ *[the preceding three sentences have been moved to paragraph 21.1]*. Examples ***of places of business covered by subparagraph e)*** are fixed places of business ***used*** solely for the purpose of advertising or for the supply of information or for scientific research or for the servicing of a patent or a know-how contract, if such activities have a preparatory or auxiliary character *[this sentence currently appears at the end of paragraph 23]*. ***Paragraph 4 would not apply, however,*** ~~This would not be the case, where, for example,~~ ***if a*** fixed place of business ***used for the supply of information would*** ~~does~~ not only give information but ***would*** also furnish~~es~~ plans etc. specially developed for the purposes of the individual customer. Nor would it ~~be the case~~ ***apply*** if a research establishment were to concern itself with manufacture *[these two sentences currently appear at the end of paragraph 25]*. ***Similarly,*** ~~W~~***w***here~~, for example,~~ the servicing of patents and know-how is the purpose of an enterprise, a fixed place of business of such enterprise exercising such an activity cannot get the benefits of ***paragraph 4*** ~~subparagraph *e)*~~. A fixed place of business which has the function of managing an enterprise or even only a part of an enterprise or of a group of the concern cannot be regarded as doing a preparatory or auxiliary activity, for such a managerial activity exceeds this level. If ***an*** enterprise~~s~~ with international ramifications establish***es*** a so-called "management office" in ***a*** State~~s~~ in which ~~they~~***it*** maintain***s*** subsidiaries, permanent establishments, agents or licensees, such office having supervisory and coordinating functions for all departments of the enterprise located within the region concerned, ***subparagraph e) will not apply to that "management office" because*** ~~a permanent establishment will normally be deemed to exist, because the management office may be regarded as an office within the meaning of paragraph 2. Where a big international concern has delegated all management functions to its regional management offices so that the functions of the head office of the concern are restricted to general supervision (so called polycentric enterprises), the regional management offices even have to be regarded as a "place of management" within the meaning of subparagraph *a)* of paragraph 2. T~~***t***he function of managing an enterprise, even if it only covers a certain area of the operations of the concern, constitutes an essential part of the business operations of the enterprise and therefore can in no way be regarded as an activity which has a preparatory or auxiliary character within the meaning of ~~subparagraph *e)* of~~ paragraph 4.

~~25. A permanent establishment could also be constituted if an enterprise maintains a fixed place of business for the delivery of spare parts to customers for machinery supplied to those customers where, in addition, it maintains or repairs such machinery, as this goes beyond the pure delivery mentioned in subparagraph *a)* of paragraph 4. Since these after sale organisations perform an essential and significant part of the services of an enterprise vis-à-vis its customers, their activities are not merely auxiliary ones. Subparagraph *e)* applies only if the activity of the fixed place of business is limited to a preparatory or auxiliary one. This would not be the case where, for example, the fixed place of business does not only give information but also furnishes plans etc. specially developed for the purposes of the individual customer. Nor would it be the case if a research establishment were to concern itself with manufacture.~~

~~26. Moreover, subparagraph *e)* makes it clear that the activities of the fixed place of business must be carried on for the enterprise. A fixed place of business which renders services not only to its enterprise but also directly to other enterprises, for example to other companies of a group to which the company owning the fixed place belongs, would not fall within the scope of subparagraph *e)*.~~

~~26.1 Another example is that of facilities such as cables or pipelines that cross the territory of a country. Apart from the fact that income derived by the owner or operator of such facilities from their use by other enterprises is covered by Article 6 where they constitute immovable property under paragraph 2 of Article 6, the question may arise as to whether paragraph 4 applies to them. Where these facilities are used to transport property belonging to other enterprises, subparagraph *a)*, which is restricted to delivery of goods or merchandise belonging to the enterprise that uses the facility, will not be applicable as concerns the owner or operator of these facilities. Subparagraph *e)* also will not be applicable as concerns that enterprise since the cable or pipeline is not used solely for the enterprise and its use is not of preparatory or auxiliary character given the nature of the business of that enterprise. The situation is different, however, where an enterprise owns and operates a cable or pipeline that crosses the territory of a country solely for purposes of transporting its own property and such transport is merely incidental to the business of that enterprise, as in the case of an enterprise that is in the business of refining oil and that owns and operates a pipeline that crosses the territory of a country solely to transport its own oil to its refinery located in another country. In such case, subparagraph *a)* would be applicable. An additional question is whether the cable or pipeline could also constitute a permanent establishment for the customer of the operator of the cable or pipeline, *i.e.* the enterprise whose data, power or property is transmitted or transported from one place to another. In such a case, the enterprise is merely obtaining transmission or transportation services provided by the operator of the cable or pipeline and does not have the cable or pipeline at its disposal. As a consequence, the cable or pipeline cannot be considered to be a permanent establishment of that enterprise.~~

27. As already mentioned in paragraph 21 above, paragraph 4 is designed to provide ~~for~~ exceptions to the general definition of paragraph 1 in respect of fixed places of business which are engaged in activities having a preparatory or auxiliary character. Therefore, according to subparagraph *f)* ~~of paragraph 4~~, the fact that one fixed place of business combines any of the activities mentioned in subparagraphs *a)* to *e)* ~~of paragraph 4~~ does not mean of itself that a permanent establishment exists. As long as the combined activity of such a fixed place of business is merely preparatory or auxiliary, a permanent establishment should be deemed not to exist. Such combinations should not be viewed on rigid lines, but should be considered in the light of the particular circumstances. ~~The criterion "preparatory or auxiliary character" is to be interpreted in the same way as is set out for the same criterion of subparagraph *e)* (see paragraphs 24 and 25 above). States which want to allow any combination of the items mentioned in subparagraphs *a)* to *e)*, disregarding whether or not the criterion of the preparatory or auxiliary character of such a combination is met, are free to do so by deleting the words "provided" to "character" in subparagraph *f)*.~~

~~27.1 Subparagraph *f)* is of no importance in a case where an enterprise maintains several fixed places of business within the meaning of subparagraphs *a)* to *e)* provided that they are separated from each other locally and organisationally, as in such a case each place of business has to be viewed separately and in isolation for deciding whether a permanent establishment exists. Places of business are not "separated organisationally" where they each perform in a Contracting State complementary functions such as receiving and storing goods in one place, distributing those goods through another etc. An enterprise cannot fragment a cohesive operating business into several small operations in order to argue that each is merely engaged in a preparatory or auxiliary activity.~~

28. The fixed places of business ~~mentioned in~~***to which*** paragraph 4 ***applies do not*** ~~cannot be deemed to~~ constitute permanent establishments so long as ~~their~~***the business*** activities ***performed through those fixed places of business*** are restricted to the ***activities referred to in that paragraph*** ~~functions which are the prerequisite for assuming that the fixed place of business is not a permanent establishment~~. This will be the case even if the contracts necessary for establishing and carrying on the***se*** business ***activities*** are concluded by those in charge of the places of business themselves. ***The conclusion of such contracts by these employees will not constitute a permanent establishment of the enterprise under*** ~~The employees of places of business within the meaning of paragraph 4 who are authorised to conclude such contracts should not be regarded as agents within the meaning of~~ paragraph 5 ***as long as the conclusion of these contracts satisfies the conditions of paragraph 4 (see paragraph 33 below)***. ~~A case in point would be a research institution~~ ***An example would be where*** the manager of ~~which~~ ***a place of business where preparatory or auxiliary research activities are conducted*** ~~of which is authorised to~~ conclude***s*** the contracts necessary for ***establishing and*** maintaining ***that place of business*** ~~the institution and who exercises this authority within the framework~~ ***as part of the activities carried on at that location*** ~~functions of the institution~~. ~~A permanent establishment, however, exists if the fixed place of business exercising any of the functions listed in paragraph 4 were to exercise them not only on behalf of the enterprise to which it belongs but also on behalf of other enterprises. If, for instance, an advertising agency maintained by an enterprise were also to engage in advertising for other enterprises, it would be regarded as a permanent establishment of the enterprise by which it is maintained.~~

29. If, ***under paragraph 4,*** a fixed place of business ~~under paragraph 4~~ is deemed not to be a permanent establishment, this exception applies likewise to the disposal of movable property forming part of the business property of the place of business at the termination of the enterprise's activity ***at that place*** ~~in such installation~~ (see paragraph 11 above and paragraph 2 of Article 13). ~~Since~~***Where***, for example, the display of merchandise during a trade fair ***or convention*** is excepted under subparagraphs *a)* and *b)*, the sale of th***at***~~e~~ merchandise at the termination of ***the***~~a~~ trade fair or convention is covered by ***subparagraph e) as such sale is merely an auxiliary activity***~~this exception~~. The exception does not, of course, apply to sales of merchandise not actually displayed at the trade fair or convention.

30. ***Where paragraph 4 does not apply because*** ***a***~~A~~ fixed place of business used ***by an enterprise*** ~~both~~ for activities ***that are listed in that*** ~~which rank as exceptions~~ ~~***of***~~ ~~(~~paragraph 4~~)~~ ***is also used*** ~~and~~ for other ***activities that go beyond what is preparatory or auxiliary, that place of business*** constitutes a single permanent establishment ***of the enterprise and the profits attributable to the permanent establishment with respect to*** ~~as regards~~ both types of activities ***may be taxed in the State where that permanent establishment is situated.*** ~~This would be the case, for instance, where a store maintained for the delivery of goods also engaged in sales.~~

30.1 Some States consider that some of the activities referred to in paragraph 4 are intrinsically preparatory or auxiliary and, in order to provide greater certainty for both tax administrations and taxpayers, take the view that these activities should not be subject to the condition that they be of a preparatory or auxiliary character, any concern about the inappropriate use of these exceptions being addressed through the provisions of paragraph 4.1. States that share that view are free to amend paragraph 4 as follows (and may also agree to delete some of the activities listed in subparagraphs a) to d) below if they consider that these activities should be subject to the preparatory or auxiliary condition in subparagraph e)):

> ***4. Notwithstanding the preceding provisions of this Article, the term "permanent establishment" shall be deemed not to include:***
>
> ***a) the use of facilities solely for the purpose of storage, display or delivery of goods or merchandise belonging to the enterprise;***
>
> ***b) the maintenance of a stock of goods or merchandise belonging to the enterprise solely for the purpose of storage, display or delivery;***
>
> ***c) the maintenance of a stock of goods or merchandise belonging to the enterprise solely for the purpose of processing by another enterprise;***
>
> ***d) the maintenance of a fixed place of business solely for the purpose of purchasing goods or merchandise or of collecting information, for the enterprise;***
>
> ***e) the maintenance of a fixed place of business solely for the purpose of carrying on, for the enterprise, any activity not listed in subparagraphs a) to d), provided that this activity has a preparatory or auxiliary character, or***
>
> ***f) the maintenance of a fixed place of business solely for any combination of activities mentioned in subparagraphs a) to e), provided that the overall activity of the fixed place of business resulting from this combination is of a preparatory or auxiliary character.***

2. *Fragmentation of activities between closely related parties*

14. Paragraph 27.1 of the Commentary on Article 5 currently deals with the application of Art. 5(4)*f*) in the case of what has been referred to as the "fragmentation of activities":

> 27.1 Subparagraph *f*) is of no importance in a case where an enterprise maintains several fixed places of business within the meaning of subparagraphs *a*) to *e*) provided that they are separated from each other locally and organisationally, as in such a case each place of business has to be viewed separately and in isolation for deciding whether a permanent establishment exists. Places of business are not "separated organisationally" where they each perform in a Contracting State complementary functions such as receiving and storing goods in one place, distributing those goods through another etc. An enterprise cannot fragment a cohesive operating business into several small operations in order to argue that each is merely engaged in a preparatory or auxiliary activity.

15. Given the ease with which subsidiaries may be established, the logic of the last sentence ("[a]n enterprise cannot fragment a cohesive operating business into several small operations in order to argue that each is merely engaged in a preparatory or auxiliary activity") should not be restricted to cases where the same enterprise maintains different places of business in a country but should be extended to cases where these places of business belong to closely related enterprises. Some BEPS concerns related to Art. 5(4) will therefore be addressed by the rule proposed below which will take account not only of the activities carried on by the same enterprise at different places but also of the activities carried on by closely related enterprises at different places or at the same place. This new rule is the logical consequence of the decision to restrict the scope of Art. 5(4) to activities that have a "preparatory and auxiliary" character because, in the absence of that rule, it would be relatively easy to use closely related enterprises in order to segregate activities which, when taken together, go beyond that threshold.

NEW ANTI-FRAGMENTATION RULE

Add the following new paragraph 4.1 to Article 5:

> ***4.1 Paragraph 4 shall not apply to a fixed place of business that is used or maintained by an enterprise if the same enterprise or a closely related enterprise carries on business activities at the same place or at another place in the same Contracting State and***
>
> ***a) that place or other place constitutes a permanent establishment for the enterprise or the closely related enterprise under the provisions of this Article, or***
>
> ***b) the overall activity resulting from the combination of the activities carried on by the two enterprises at the same place, or by the same enterprise or closely related enterprises at the two places, is not of a preparatory or auxiliary character,***
>
> ***provided that the business activities carried on by the two enterprises at the same place, or by the same enterprise or closely related enterprises at the two places, constitute complementary functions that are part of a cohesive business operation.***

Proposed changes to the Commentary on Article 5 (changes to the existing text of the Commentary appear in bold italics for additions and strikethrough for deletions)

Replace existing paragraph 27.1 of the Commentary on Article 5 by the following:

27.1 ***Unless the anti-fragmentation provisions of paragraph 4.1 are applicable (see below),*** ~~S~~subparagraph *f)* is of no importance in a case where an enterprise maintains several fixed places of business within the meaning of subparagraphs *a)* to *e)* ~~provided that they are separated from each other locally and organisationally,~~ as in such a case each place of business has to be viewed separately and in isolation for deciding whether a permanent establishment exists. ~~Places of business are not "separated organisationally" where they each perform in a Contracting State complementary functions such as receiving and storing goods in one place, distributing those goods through another etc. An enterprise cannot fragment a cohesive operating business into several small operations in order to argue that each is merely engaged in a preparatory or auxiliary activity.~~

Add the following new paragraphs to the Commentary on Article 5:

Paragraph 4.1

30.2 The purpose of paragraph 4.1 is to prevent an enterprise or a group of closely related enterprises from fragmenting a cohesive business operation into several small operations in order to argue that each is merely engaged in a preparatory or auxiliary activity. Under paragraph 4.1, the exceptions provided for by paragraph 4 do not apply to a place of business that would otherwise constitute a permanent establishment where the activities carried on at that place and other activities of the same enterprise or of closely related enterprises exercised at that place or at another place in the same State constitute complementary functions that are part of a cohesive business operation. For paragraph 4.1 to apply, however, at least one of the places where these activities are exercised must constitute a permanent establishment or, if that is not the case, the overall activity resulting from the combination of the relevant activities must go beyond what is merely preparatory or auxiliary.

30.3 The concept of "closely related enterprises" that is used in paragraph 4.1 is defined in subparagraph b) of paragraph 6 of the Article (see paragraphs 38.8 to 38.10 below).

30.4 The following examples illustrate the application of paragraph 4.1:

- ***Example A: RCO, a bank resident of State R, has a number of branches in State S which constitute permanent establishments. It also has a separate office in State S where a few employees verify information provided by clients that have made loan applications at these different branches. The results of the verifications done by the employees are forwarded to the headquarters of RCO in State R where other employees analyse the information included in the loan applications and provide reports to the branches where the decisions to grant the loans are made. In that case, the exceptions of paragraph 4 will not apply to the office because another place (i.e. any of the other branches where the loan applications are made) constitutes a permanent establishment of RCO in State S*** *and the business activities carried on by RCO at the office and at the relevant branch constitute complementary functions that are part of a cohesive business operation (i.e. providing loans to clients in State S).*

– *Example B: RCO, a company resident of State R, manufactures and sells appliances. SCO, a resident of State S that is a wholly-owned subsidiary of RCO, owns a store where it sells appliances that it acquires from RCO. RCO also owns a small warehouse in State S where it stores a few large items that are identical to some of those displayed in the store owned by SCO. When a customer buys such a large item from SCO, SCO employees go to the warehouse where they take possession of the item before delivering it to the customer; the ownership of the item is only acquired by SCO from RCO when the item leaves the warehouse. In this case, paragraph 4.1 prevents the application of the exceptions of paragraph 4 to the warehouse and it will not be necessary, therefore, to determine whether paragraph 4, and in particular subparagraph 4 a), applies to the warehouse. The conditions for the application of paragraph 4.1 are met because*

- *SCO and RCO are closely related enterprises;*
- *SCO's store constitutes a permanent establishment of SCO (the definition of permanent establishment is not limited to situations where a resident of one Contracting State uses or maintains a fixed place of business in the other State; it applies equally where an enterprise of one State uses or maintains a fixed place of business in that same State); and*
- *The business activities carried on by RCO at its warehouse and by SCO at its store constitute complementary functions that are part of a cohesive business operation (i.e. storing goods in one place for the purpose of delivering these goods as part of the obligations resulting from the sale of these goods through another place in the same State).*

C. Other strategies for the artificial avoidance of PE status

1. Splitting-up of contracts

16. The splitting-up of contracts in order to abuse the exception in paragraph 3 of Article 5 is discussed in paragraph 18 of the Commentary on Art. 5:

> 18. … The twelve month threshold has given rise to abuses; it has sometimes been found that enterprises (mainly contractors or subcontractors working on the continental shelf or engaged in activities connected with the exploration and exploitation of the continental shelf) divided their contracts up into several parts, each covering a period less than twelve months and attributed to a different company which was, however, owned by the same group. Apart from the fact that such abuses may, depending on the circumstances, fall under the application of legislative or judicial anti-avoidance rules, countries concerned with this issue can adopt solutions in the framework of bilateral negotiations.

17. The Principal Purposes Test (PPT) rule that will be added to the OECD Model Tax Convention as a result of the adoption of the Report on Action 6 (*Preventing the Granting of Treaty Benefits in Inappropriate Circumstances*)[3] will address the BEPS concerns related to the abusive splitting-up of contracts. In order to make this clear, the following example will be added to the Commentary on the PPT rule. For States that are unable to address the issue through domestic anti-abuse rules, a more automatic rule will also be included in the Commentary as a provision that should be used in treaties that would not include the PPT or as an alternative provision to be used by countries specifically concerned with the splitting-up of contracts issue.

CHANGES DEALING WITH THE SPLITTING-UP OF CONTRACTS

1. Add the following example to the Commentary on the PPT rule proposed in the Report on Action 6:

Example J: RCo is a company resident of State R. It has successfully submitted a bid for the construction of a power plant for SCO, an independent company resident of State S. That construction project is expected to last 22 months. During the negotiation of the contract, the project is divided into two different contracts, each lasting 11 months. The first contract is concluded with RCO and the second contract is concluded with SUBCO, a recently incorporated wholly-owned subsidiary of RCO resident of State R. At the request of SCO, which wanted to ensure that RCO would be contractually liable for the performance of the two contracts, the contractual arrangements are such that RCO is jointly and severally liable with SUBCO for the performance of SUBCO's contractual obligations under the SUBCO-SCO contract.

In this example, in the absence of other facts and circumstances showing otherwise, it would be reasonable to conclude that one of the principal purposes for the conclusion of the separate contract under which SUBCO agreed to perform part of the construction project was for RCO and SUBCO to each obtain the benefit of the rule in paragraph 3 of Article 5 of the State R-State S tax convention. Granting the benefit of that rule in these circumstances would be contrary to the object and purpose of that paragraph as the time limitation of that paragraph would otherwise be meaningless.

2. *Replace paragraph 18 of the Commentary on paragraph 3 of Article 5 by the following (consequential changes will be required to paragraphs 42.45-42.48 of the Commentary):*

18. The twelve month test applies to each individual site or project. In determining how long the site or project has existed, no account should be taken of the time previously spent by the contractor concerned on other sites or projects which are totally unconnected with it. A building site should be regarded as a single unit, even if it is based on several contracts, provided that it forms a coherent whole commercially and geographically. Subject to this proviso, a building site forms a single unit even if the orders have been placed by several persons (e.g. for a row of houses). *[rest of the paragraph is moved to paragraph 18.1]*

18.1 The twelve month threshold has given rise to abuses; it has sometimes been found that enterprises (mainly contractors or subcontractors working on the continental shelf or engaged in activities connected with the exploration and exploitation of the continental shelf) divided their contracts up into several parts, each covering a period of less than twelve months and attributed to a different company which was, however, owned by the same group. Apart from the fact that such abuses may, depending on the circumstances, fall under the application of legislative or judicial anti-avoidance rules, ~~countries concerned with this issue can adopt solutions in the framework of bilateral negotiations.~~ ***these abuses could also be addressed through the application of the anti-abuse rule of paragraph 7 of Article [X], as shown by example J in paragraph [14] of the Commentary on Article [X]. Some States may nevertheless wish to deal expressly with such abuses. Moreover, States that do not include paragraph 7 of Article [X] in their treaties should include an additional provision to address contract splitting. Such a provision could, for example, be drafted along the following lines:***

> ***For the sole purpose of determining whether the twelve month period referred to in paragraph 3 has been exceeded,***
>
> ***a) where an enterprise of a Contracting State carries on activities in the other Contracting State at a place that constitutes a building site or construction or installation project and these activities are carried on during periods of time that do not last more than twelve months, and***
>
> ***b) connected activities are carried on at the same building site or construction or installation project during different periods of time, each exceeding 30 days, by one or more enterprises closely related to the first-mentioned enterprise,***
>
> ***these different periods of time shall be added to the period of time during which the first-mentioned enterprise has carried on activities at that building site or construction or installation project.***

The concept of "closely related enterprises" that is used in the above provision is defined in subparagraph b) of paragraph 6 of the Article (see paragraphs 38.8 to 38.10 below).

18.2 For the purposes of the alternative provision found in paragraph 18.1, the determination of whether activities are connected will depend on the facts and circumstances of each case. Factors that may especially be relevant for that purpose include:

- ***whether the contracts covering the different activities were concluded with the same person or related persons;***

- ***whether the conclusion of additional contracts with a person is a logical consequence of a previous contract concluded with that person or related persons;***
- ***whether the activities would have been covered by a single contract absent tax planning considerations;***
- ***whether the nature of the work involved under the different contracts is the same or similar;***
- ***whether the same employees are performing the activities under the different contracts.***

2. Strategies for selling insurance in a State without having a PE therein

18. As part of the work on Action 7, BEPS concerns related to situations where a large network of exclusive agents is used to sell insurance for a foreign insurer were also examined. It was ultimately concluded, however, that it would be inappropriate to try to address these concerns through a PE rule that would treat insurance differently from other types of businesses and that BEPS concerns that may arise in cases where a large network of exclusive agents is used to sell insurance for a foreign insurer should be addressed through the more general changes to Art. 5(5) and 5(6) in section A of this report.

D. Profit attribution to PEs and interaction with action points on transfer pricing

19. The work on Action 7 that was done with respect to attribution of profit issues focussed on whether the existing rules of Art. 7 of the OECD Model Tax Convention would be appropriate for determining the profits that would be allocated to PEs resulting from the changes included in this report. The conclusion of that work is that these changes do not require substantive modifications to the existing rules and guidance concerning the attribution of profits to a permanent establishment under Article 7 but that there is a need for additional guidance on how the rules of Article 7 would apply to PEs resulting from the changes in this report, in particular for PEs outside the financial sector. There is also a need to take account of the results of the work on other parts of the BEPS Action Plan dealing with transfer pricing, in particular the work related to intangibles, risk and capital.

20. Realistically, however, work on attribution of profit issues related to Action 7 could not be undertaken before the work on Action 7 and Actions 8-10 had been completed. For that reason, and based on the many comments that have stressed the need for additional guidance on the issue of attribution of profits to PEs, follow-up work on attribution of profits issues related to Action 7 will be carried on after September 2015 with a view to providing the necessary guidance before the end of 2016, which is the deadline for the negotiation of the multilateral instrument that will implement the results of the work on treaty issues mandated by the BEPS Action Plan.

Notes

1 See paragraph 14 of the Commentary on the PPT rule included in paragraph 26 of that Report.

2 See www.oecd.org/tax/treaties/48836726.pdf (2011 discussion draft) and www.oecd.org/ctp/treaties/PermanentEstablishment.pdf (2012 discussion draft).

3 See paragraph 14 of the Commentary on the PPT rule included in paragraph 26 of the Report on Action 6.

Bibliography

OECD (2015a), *Preventing the Granting of Treaty Benefits in Inappropriate Circumstances, Action 6 - 2015 Final Report*, OECD/G20 Base Erosion and Profit Shifting Project, OECD Publishing, Paris, http://dx.doi.org/10.1787/9789264241695-en.

OECD (2015b), *Addressing the Tax Challenges of the Digital Economy, Action 1 - 2015 Final Report*, OECD/G20 Base Erosion and Profit Shifting Project, OECD Publishing, Paris, http://dx.doi.org/10.1787/9789264241046-en.

OECD (2014), *Model Tax Convention on Income and on Capital: Condensed Version 2014*, OECD Publishing, Paris, http://dx.doi.org/10.1787/mtc_cond-2014-en.

OECD (2013a), *Action Plan on Base Erosion and Profit Shifting*, OECD Publishing, Paris, http://dx.doi.org/10.1787/9789264202719-en.

OECD (2013b), *Addressing Base Erosion and Profit Shifting*, OECD Publishing, Paris, http://dx.doi.org/10.1787/9789264192744-en.

ORGANISATION FOR ECONOMIC CO-OPERATION AND DEVELOPMENT

The OECD is a unique forum where governments work together to address the economic, social and environmental challenges of globalisation. The OECD is also at the forefront of efforts to understand and to help governments respond to new developments and concerns, such as corporate governance, the information economy and the challenges of an ageing population. The Organisation provides a setting where governments can compare policy experiences, seek answers to common problems, identify good practice and work to co-ordinate domestic and international policies.

The OECD member countries are: Australia, Austria, Belgium, Canada, Chile, the Czech Republic, Denmark, Estonia, Finland, France, Germany, Greece, Hungary, Iceland, Ireland, Israel, Italy, Japan, Korea, Luxembourg, Mexico, the Netherlands, New Zealand, Norway, Poland, Portugal, the Slovak Republic, Slovenia, Spain, Sweden, Switzerland, Turkey, the United Kingdom and the United States. The European Union takes part in the work of the OECD.

OECD Publishing disseminates widely the results of the Organisation's statistics gathering and research on economic, social and environmental issues, as well as the conventions, guidelines and standards agreed by its members.

OECD PUBLISHING, 2, rue André-Pascal, 75775 PARIS CEDEX 16
(23 2015 34 1 P) ISBN 978-92-64-24121-3 – 2015-01

www.ingramcontent.com/pod-product-compliance
Lightning Source LLC
LaVergne TN
LVHW081424110826
845149LV00010B/1864